MW00758249

ATM

Books published by Georgetown Review Press are available at special discounts for bulk purchases in the United States by corporations, institutions, and other organizations. For more information please contact the press at the address listed above.

Book design by Ryan Cook
Cover design by Robin Vuchnich

First Edition
ISBN-13: 978-0-615-90617-1
ISBN-10: 0-615-90617-1

Georgetown Review Press
400 East College Street, Box 227
Georgetown, KY 40324

http://georgetownreview.georgetowncollege.edu.

PREVIOUS BOOKS BY CHRISTOPHER SALERNO

Whirligig / 2006

Minimum Heroic / 2010

ACKNOWLEDGEMENTS

Poems from this manuscript have been published in: *Coconut, Boston Review, Big Bell, Coldfront, Crazyhorse, Drunken Boat, Failbetter, Fence, InDigest, LIT, Laurel Review, Sink Review,* and *Thethepoetry.com*. Some of the following poems appeared in a chapbook, *ATM*, from Horseless Press, 2011. Thank you, Jen Tynes. Others appeared in a chapbook, *Automatic Teller*, winner of the Laurel Review Midwest Chapbook prize. Thank you John Gallaher and Mary Biddinger. Thank you D.A. Powell for seeing fit to select this book. Special thanks to Timothy Liu, John Parras, Reb Livingston, Chris Tonelli, and Adam Clay—all fabulous people whose close readings and/or conversations helped me finish this book. Special thanks, also, to Ryan Cook and Robin Vuchnich for the thoughtful and careful design of this book. Thank you Steven Carter for being such an accommodating and helpful press editor. And to Jessica Rohrbach Salerno for everything else.

This book was written with the generous support of the Humanities and Social Sciences Summer Grant Program at William Paterson University. Thank you, WPU!

PART ONE

PART TWO

CONTENTS

PART THREE

CONTENTS

*A sudden light transfigures a trivial thing, a weather-vane,
a wind-mill, a winnowing flail, the dust in the barn door; a
moment, and the thing has vanished, because it was pure effect;
but it leaves a relish behind it, a longing that the accident may
happen again.*

Walter Pater

*In New York I am to be disenfranchised, and in New Jersey
hanged. You will not…conclude that I have become disposed to
submit tamely to the machinations of a banditti.*

Aaron Burr

PART ONE

$

I hope you like black comedy.
The black market in the rain.

The blue jay chasing the catbird
and the catbird disappearing.

This morning I woke to a radio
show about soldiers' prosthesis,

that semi-realistic look. Maybe
the word was prothesis,

from the Greeks, for the laying
out of a body after death.

I hope not. As Longinus says,
few annunciations are complete

thoughts. Language only blows
a thought apart, says Aristotle.

If you can hear this thought
you are inside a minor elegy

after a war. The black market
is filling with treasures.

12:52PM | 9/30/12 | WTHDRWL

In line behind a lady, my automatic distance
(to her, the curb

behind me, the bank parking lot
full of cars)—

we are relearning arrangement
and remainder.

That all remaining choices are either physical
or financial—

the money inside the money alive.
I approach the ATM's outer shell. Stand there.

It comes up
to my liver. The chambers of the heart

and lungs polish the breath.
I smell the wet wood chips off the path.

Here comes
my old supervisor with hail on his coat.

It's warmer now, the planet.
We wait for the wonderful machine to cough

up my balance. I want to be
automatically the only one alive.

I notice a large robin
egg on the sidewalk—

near the building, some tulips open
too wide to go on living.

SALVO

Some of the dead were known to you.
You arrange your arms to atone.

You arrange your hair like
someone about to atone.

To atone you pay seventy-five dollars
for orthopedic shoes.

To bed you wear scrubs
hoping to sweat out what allowed you to live.

You play your records, dance more.
Your upper lip gets stronger.

But all your records are thrift.
By morning, their liner notes curl

and brown in the sunlight. This is how
things bargain their way

away from you.
In every tree, a paperback book.

This is forgiveness negated.
This is the paperback book negating

the hardback.
Nothing super-historical changes.

The blood you take is equal to
the blood you make.

$$

Danger, please hold my wallet and keys / at least
for the brief time we are together / I have to be
somewhere else in this house / there are heavy
metal records in the basement / one with a panther
on the cover / a man screaming / at men like
the blare of chrysanthemums / in the long patch
of dirt beside the stoop / what impulse allows
most fully is a loss / to be misremembered / upstairs
I can no longer describe / gargoyles without
cocaine / without the previous / two decades
decades are like / basements / rectilinear with a small
industrious workshop in the back / my great-granddad
hanged himself / in his / my granddad had to cut
the body down / they were both
sort of old at that point.

9:12PM | 6/19/12 | WTHDRWL

The magnolia near the bank
is full of hornets. A beautiful blonde runs

back to her car with money.
No one has ever named this procedure.

Reader, you can see
in my mouth the sum of my wallet,

this sense of the world
as souvenir. I sometimes make withdrawals

just for the tautology.
If the sun is made up of millions

of zeros, then it cannot be made
of billions of hornets.

It's after dark. The Asian markets are in ecstasy.
The ancient Chinese poems

are full of certainty. They say love
all transactions, put aside the world.

$

Slept in headphones, dreamed of Henry
Thoreau with coke on his nose.

There is no way of firewalling dreams
from the excesses of dreams.

I went to the woods for business purposes.
To redefine the word "afford."

What is more beautiful than the future
perfect tense deadening

all questions before they arise? I want to tell you
about a wager I made (for a case

of Cote du Rhone) that future human
beings will have no regulations

beyond their facial expressions. Possibly all
we'll have is the pale sensation

of a debt coming due.
I will be brief: One dollar twenty cents

for mini-donuts. Dollar twenty
pack of yellow gum. Two-dollar large

Walden Pond postcard.
The holes in the postcard are for your oars.

$$

Today my face is a Walden Pond.
My poems make the errors

Thoreau called "extravagance"
or "walking off the path."

To possess literalness like a camera
lens pumping itself full

of light. Today my face is
a forest between two powerplants.

In the forest in the forest
a large fern grows like a small

business. The small business
sentence diagrams itself, finds

its own direct object: *Disownership,*
says the pond. *What goes on*

in you? Your heart, it's not divine.
Sometime around noon I remove

what is of no consequence
from my wallet, place it

in the crotch of a tree.
I stuff my wallet with leaves.

CARD NO: XXXX-XXXX-XXXX-4340

When I bank inside the bank, even hurry is lovely.
I am never married.

I am in an unfinished video starring money.
In the glass doors, I see myself

mattering. An unavoidable foil.
I want *deposit* to be different

from deposit, but the pace of our transactions
slows without comparison. My money is

always hiding. And yet my voice
withdraws in its presence.

$

Suppose
I had fallen in

love with civil
obedience

having expected
NYPD

on horseback
locked

in position like
an interest

rate guarantee
and I obey

of course
loan terminology

like a star
one can be poor

and stay alive

perpetually
in form

but underneath
become a spector

enter any
where for free

parade
in any direction

like a horse-
drawn hearse

bathed in
sunlight.

CARD NO: XXXX-XXXX-XXXX-4340

I fold my checks into origami cranes.
I never tire of taking my cash

into the bright street. I use a non-branch walk-up
but withdraw three times the amount

then walk, card in teeth, reading my receipt,
not exactly toward the car. Sometimes

I bring my wallet to a field
where under a tree with pastel leaves

a swing is hung. I ride it
from where I am to where I'm not.

IN PRODUCTION

1.

I will film and you will star.
You decide not to dye your

hair for the shoot. We see
you walking. The office park

woods are silent. A few geese
standing in spring snow. People

are gone. I switch lenses
for matters of scale. The film

happens outside of the film.
A dog coming up to you

and the security guard's car.
I carry snowballs in a bag

from Saks. Mom, there is no-
thing like working. When I

shout ACTION, you tear
your coat open making wings.

2.

How do you direct a mom
waking up? She agrees to act

in my low-fi film. At least
for ten frames in the park.

Nineteen Ninety One. I know
you're not listening.

Daisies bloom their pussy-
ass mouths. The park is occupied

by swans that all live
together. The poem speaks softly—

I mean the film. Our VCR
gives everyone green

eyes, green tongues. I crave
flavored ice in the sun. So many

things I want to film. A gorgeous
dead swan on its back.

3.

A different demographic
this morning in the park

because of the strike.
We write out the ending:

who will speak, will have spoken.
I film two white terriers discovering

a GAP bag full of plums,
an ambulance dazzling

gradually. What really happens
is something's destroyed

the focal length. Near
is now really far. This is how

the sun whitens objects
dramatically. Some light you

can't work with, is so
overly confessional.

Look at me, I can't tell
what's deluxe anymore.

4.

Some nouns   so what   no syntax   anymore

lull/lol   the ducks   interrupting   the mayflies

at rest   on wavelets   you hear   in movies   *places*

everyone, places   I did that   then a man   mother   was standing

in our sideyard   a news   helicopter sort of   hovering

overhead   that summer dad   sent me iron-on

patches from all   over the country   even one   from our town

5.

An economy still
in recovery

I trap ants in Dixie
Cups with sugar

packets and spit
a beam of light

I am not the one
waving goodbye

I'll rehearse with you
another scene

it's you die and all
your clothes

go to Goodwill
all at once.

6.

I could sell subscriptions
to my mother's dream

of moving
the peonies around

the park
her hand leaves

her silver hair
all the money in the world

My Mother
My Mahler

we won't do this again
on film

tears

on a white

silk

blouse.

IN THE QUIETEST WORLD

Camping out
I woke with a penny

stuck to my thigh
walked to the river

bank to pee
and squint at hawks

adrift like chunks
of brunette hair

it was hot I thought
I'd tan like a penny

not char like the center
of a sunflower.

WE ARE GOING SOMEWHERE

1.

We are going somewhere, somewhere important like the U.S. Mint.
In the future, we'll speak of our class trips as "neoclassical."
I can no longer visit the Liberty Bell.
Does anyone else have generalized anxiety?
General George Washington once wrote, "The man who fails
is drunk on something else."
We have all these different versions of time.
Beside the Coke machine I see a couple
having a whisper fight. I pretend
to inflate my hand like a latex glove.
Their whisper fight smells like gum.

2.

We are going somewhere, somewhere important like a fort.

Sure, I've often thought of enlisting.

But as the great Alexander Hamilton once wrote, "Money retarded me."

Rightness is not the point anymore.

At the fort some kids are playing MERCY in the grass.

There are either rules or laws (not both).

Somewhere in the fort is a bedroom for what must be a very restless type of sleep.

Outside there are twelve gates designed to make the enemy think.

Around the fort is a lot of blue water.

I trouble the water.

3.

We are going somewhere, somewhere important like a crime scene.

Perfect, a convenience store robbery.

When it involves a death, a crime scene becomes like a museum.

In this metaphor, art is the escape a criminal makes.

This poem makes escaping death worth it.

A robbery where no death occurs is a "successful" robbery.

On my way downtown I see ants carrying pieces of chateaubriand.

The ants are getting away with burglary!

The ants are where nobody thinks to look.

The ants are like a marching band routed around a wildfire.

4.

We are going somewhere, somewhere important like a Hall of Fame.

I was reading about Marianne Moore's

stroke after throwing out the first-pitch at Yankee Stadium.

There's a kind of intermediacy to the golden age of anything.

In 1909, the great Benjamin Franklin Shibe

was issued a patent for a white ball full of wool yarn.

I pretend to care less about baseball.

Marianne Moore's father died after failing to invent the smokeless furnace.

Some people are in pain in this world.

In 1992, M. Teasdale was issued the patent for Goldschlager,

a liqueur full of suspended flakes of gold.

Dear work,

       I could stay
awake for days

       word up

in my mouth

                  moon

       over the credit

       union
            all alone.

PART TWO

UPON COMPLETING A CIRCUIT

Suddenly my town is a flea market
at which I cannot find my father.

This isn't funny to the elderly.
Tomorrow is Easter. I have questions

for everyone. I'm wearing the new
AFC Championship hoodie. I purchase

two geodes straight from "mine" country.
I make no efforts to live within

my means. Muse over money spent,
but linger on the debt and it grows.

I don't know if others have their fathers.
Perhaps there is no real mystery

here at all. The disappearance of anyone
I just realized is like a short lecture

on completing a circuit. Followed by
another on how to reanimate

a demon. Followed by another
on rates of exchange. Followed by

the one that brings on night.

BYRONIC METHOD

It's going to be an interesting life.
The paper lamps are what I love.
I hope the woman reading the book
in my lap doesn't ever close it.
Even if the tips of her fingers turn black
I want to remember how her arms
make room for wings, rather than flanks.
I'm in my socks. She turns
the page, slightly tearing the top.
It's a story about feeling like you're falling
backwards off a moving train, and how
later everyone has a drink
and laughs about it. She has done this
before—read a player a book.
I close my eyes and picture her train
idling in my street. Outside, the leaves
of poplars, large pulmonary leaves
lie on the ground, the end.

Probably the world was once deluxe. Every city worth
seeing at least once. Beside the bus stop an empty
purse is starting to fill with rain.
People are dressed as if everything is circulating
outside of their clothing. On the bus
a lady reaches into the pocket of her red smock,
retrieves a Scrabble piece.
Probably the unused things have meaning.
Probably some new meaning on the downlow.
We must be nearing Newark. Everything's falling
into my heart. This poem is
an effort to sew a small band on the arm and wear it
on the last DeCamp bus to Port
Authority. No one else seeks this conceit and yet
here it is. My bus cuts through
a chill space of few imperatives. A scribble
above the seats reads, *Occupy your mouth with my cock.*

TERMS

Each car here'll
now drive

to the toll basket
(a money hole

shaped like a zero)
and do so just

for Connecticut.
One car up

a fly freaks
inside a tail light.

I get Ovid.
No one knows

all the laws.

SWEAR JAR

I placed a jar in the number one country
in the world. A pretty street I forget the name.

Banjo and guitar play on the radio.
I feel the Blues bang and expand. Volume

is continually at issue. My neighbor says
there's a fiscal cliff. My neighbor's house

is wrapped in Tyvek. Mine remains unrevised.
A yellow house on a painted road where

I sit between childbirth and nobody works.
My mind wanders like the newly dead

mother who doesn't want to be dead. It's hard
to remember, *Only be gentle with people.*

I ask god to handle my mother
like nothing else in Tennessee. I slide the jar

over my head like a helmet. I hear a police
helicopter hovering. The criminals

of the world slip past me. I've forgotten
to wear my orthotics. I walk in

the enormity. I drop one shoulder
like a zombie. I'm down, again, about money.

10:14PM | 6/18/12 | WTHDRWL

What else happens to the customer at night?
I was thinking of my mother, thin

from my every demand for food.
If I'd learned Polish I could explain.

She used a separate language in the stores
buying pints of duck blood soup.

A fat boy, I sat and ate a soft pear. Its seeds
rose up in me like seeds. How

do I explain? Craving flavored ice in the sun.
Plucking the marigolds next to the bank.

I watched my mother, body like a cello,
walk her weird tears around. Tonight

I am hungry for chateaubriand, yellow
squash, words and music. The long fermata

held and held. Those nothing-happening
parts of the noise of the world

begin like a podcast at night. After the sun
goes behind the book. I imagine *this,* but not that.

I have a cello to pawn. Tied together, its strings
would stretch into the dining room.

When my mother dies I will play a song
no one's ears have ever heard.

Not even the ears of my real father. Or
I could sell the cello to you. I'll pack the cello

in the heads of marigolds. I'll send with it
a tiny portrait of my mother stenciled

on a piece of pine bark mulch:
her back to you, her face to the ATM.

4′ 33″

I hope you like documentaries. Never mind
what about. In Newsweek I highlight "cochlear

atrophy" in an article about the inner ear
of different species. I'm letting the day trans-

form into symptoms. If you concentrate you can
hear the gnashing of your eyelids. Anyway

the world thinks you've gone to sleep, foregoing
I can't remember what—but do not hum it.

I have to tell you this because—lying supine
in the yellow grass, wires composing evening above

a stand of pines, a car that wont start—
when my father died, music became actual

for awhile. Until the need to hear him disappeared.
I let the forgetting begin with bell-sounds,

then more Foxtrot music than a person can use.
When the arm swings back in place after playing

a 78, there's the adamancy of growing older
for a minute, then the sounds of our same forever.

UPTICK

Moderate to heavy trading today
on fears of another Greece.

There is pathos in the sound
of things, a typo in the new

mural next to the square.
Today, an earthquake has ruined

the birthplace of Grover
Cleveland. The town might be

in agony but I don't think so.
Some people out at sunset cross the street

and are all gold. The mayor says
there is no other peril

there is just this peril. There is what
the instrument can register

and only that. If the heart of poetry
is I buy batteries

to banish a thought, I banish
the thought. Climb stairs

to rise. Look through my
grandmother's opera glasses

at the steeple, see that it is shaking
from an aftershock. I am no

surrealist but every memory
to me has a dial.

IN THE COMMERCIAL
THEY ARE FLYING

One hot air
balloon overtakes

another.
Someone sabers

a bottle of champagne.
The sky is glossy

photography for everyone
up there. Is it safe

again to spend?
Object, please verb

and come back all different.
Be a big comb

passing through
everything I now own

until this life of things of mine
is sifted

for a brief moment
from the sky

gorging on scale. Like dots
so far away

they never move.

Ballooners, lower yourselves:

The fundamentals
of the economy are strong.

HAVING THE TALK

I see pretty
far away with my glasses.
The color of
minor birds when light
comes. Strain
leaves people thinner,
has its season. Time
for specifics. I pause
in the middle of
the street for a bee
passing on its way
to a blossom—
one that is deep
and pink.

CHING

My D student says it's always nighttime in her notebook. Or else it's winter.
Her idea to protect the line
was mine. She plucks lint from my sweater and I do little more than act
like a boss, perfectly obese. I tell her to
stop for a second, diagram
this sentence about myopia: *An / orange / Skittle / lay /on / the / sticky /floor.*
I elevate my voice so we don't fall asleep. I try buying
more candy. The coins are new
and like little mirrors. I put in all nickels
but nothing comes out.

LESS AND LESS IS NOT A
TRANSACTION

I want to be the branch manager
who never takes lunch
who lets everyone touch
the rectangular molds for money.
It's time to think like a mint.
This definition of where
things come from speaks to
the world as a made place. Ask me
when I first noticed my own
negative thinking. I tell you
in these sentences:
A tree outlives its welcome.
A poem doesn't mean what it says
if it includes a sweepstakes.
I've been staring out the window
at everyone's clouds. Still
the urge to own a convertible,
gone the urge to grow
my own food, to go into the woods
with my bankbook.
I sit in the groin of a large tree
probably being seen
by the neighbors. Let's take a walk
to the candle factory.
The barrels of wax over
which bats drift

at dusk is fantastic.
This is how we judge things
before they exist,
and how buying
a thing erases it. I bought
an unscented candle, it tipped
over in the night burning
up the bottom of my bed sheet
until I put the flames
out with seltzer and returned
to sleep only to be
awakened later by coins
dropping, the sound of dial-up
connecting everyone
electronically at sunrise.
Awake, I see a cat with snow
on its back. I watch a squirrel plow
a branch of snow. Am I
to believe squirrels don't place
tiny bets against each other?
What, in finance,
isn't fetishistic? Right now it's like
I'm with friends, breathing
and thinking less. I'm pouring out
my free refill, getting city water
from the sink. All of this
meditating on money returning
to everyone's hands—

these things happen and
I'm reminded of the creased lines
in the trunk of our apartment's elm,
the tiny courtyard in which
a retired greyhound sits
like a non-flying bird
beside the Mountain
Dew machine. If only I could go
where my dimes go. If only
I could stop saying
whole 'nother day, as if days
were nothing but daydreams.
Of a gray coin worn smooth
from a bazillion transactions.
I turn the coin over and
here comes heads.

8:42ΛM | 10/16/12 | WTHDRWL

Finally, I could lay down one mile
of business cards, stop
needing peoples' names repeated.
Outside, the blue Toyota
hood melting flurries. It happens
that remembrance works
best in vengeance. I look
for patterns. Chipmunks
run away from winter
while I walk. Again, I turn uphill
and to the right. Here
is the road. I'm satisfied
to find a hubcap someone else has lost—
the just-cosmetic edge of
something insular.

11:12PM | 9/22/12 | WTHDRWL

No one is alive
except someone in a bowtie

withdrawals his life savings
in the rain.

Rain collects
in his medical device.

Rain collects somehow
in the holes

where things used to be.
We're not afraid.

There is something gentle
about the daisy chain

of white receipts
the ATM will feed the world.

A billboard stretches out
above my head.

Two crows on its catwalk
urgently mate.

A ladybug hits the ATM and falls
to the ground.

Goodnight, bruise.
Every vision is a bargain.

Bougainvillea,
I stand here and look at you

and pay nothing.

PART THREE

MEASUREMENT INC.

At long last, a bronze age.
An invoice on the clear glass desk.
An earth so flat I coast forever.
I tell you all I love this job.
When office supplies arrive, every
thing gets stapled down,
becomes part of the natural
configuration. Even birds outside
incorporate on the ground.
Now I quit this job and give it to you.
Imagine yourself scoring
tests for state governments, locating
error, explicating student doubt.
Do you have a dream?
In my cubicle dream there
are something like a dozen Tony
Hawks flying over me and
hitting the mirrored windowglass.
The critical reflection eludes
the critical function of flight.
What kind of hawk would you be
and why? Do you think
there are echoes inside of eggs?
I know I know one thing:
you are much better than me
at ornithology
where a question is always
being raised and never answered.

$

I can't be any more real than I just was.
I had just taken a big drink when an ambulance went by
in the too-wet snow. The order of things
is vulgar—the ongoing winter, its unquotable weather
wants me to pop.
Approximately an inch of snow lay on the neighbor's trampoline.
It draws tight like a conga.
Hundreds of birds interpret this.
An interrogative sentence wells up inside me. I don't know how
small my problems are.
I only profit when there is nothing
to turn into for money.

$$

People are getting free shipping, and all the bees are gone.
Last frost, I guess. I can't describe another spring
without touching everything still here.
And it hurts me to do it. The vacant hive
has that triggered look.
I keep dreaming of a bee hole,
a whole lung full of bees I'd like to move away from.
To begin a journey most people stand up,
fold the map, pretend not to need it,
then falter into bushes, too near dying, barely moving lips—
can I stop this March?
I was going to say something about my own mom,
the physical hive of her head pulsing out.
She hasn't studied the drowsy inflections of bees.
I wish an armored car would go by.

$$$

People were getting 10% off. We could see
the place to grind the beans.
On the far end of the store a wall of televisions
tuned to one channel:
footage of a high-speed chase north of Dallas.
Big distance. To say the sale
is in me. To then not mean it.
I keep thinking
I need staples for the gun.
I don't. I push the cart
to my car. My silver watch scatters light.

RISE, FORTUNE

Lost, I check the time on my receipt,
let it guide my walk. At what point does a memory
rob the new of its newness?
There is a yogurt lid in the mud (not mine).
I walk and walk
until I reach the stores.
I wait in long lines. Flicking my lighter
I slightly burn a girl's braids. The smoke
is sweet like popsicle,
though sweet for us depends
on our following the flame
into the dim. Forget what I've said
about being lost. I love.

CARD NO: XXXX-XXXX-XXXX-9910

A found wallet can also be a book to help me fall asleep.
The end is sad, if you think about it.
First I take his dollars out, condition them in the sink.
The stiffness of cash and maps
likely helps them to last. But money must rely on
my hunger for sneakers and wordlessness
or move over. The sun's light
on the other side of the house now—
can you still here the squeak of the world?
This book should end
with a wallet to the throat
of someone older.

REFINERY

For the trains they made miles of something
and then the perfect platform
for an imperative sentence.
Above me flows a river,
harbor and bilge. I'm in love with
Port Authority.
In the urinal I take out
my master card.

12:52PM | 10/30/12 | DEPOSIT

I'd like to start again. I'm not learning
to preserve energy or predict

what the Dow will do. Can I say *fuck*
this season? I halt my jog, unzip my

jacket, walk awhile backwards
near the bank where someone's left a Coke

bottle in the crook of a tree.
Each spring brings distillation, perfume

and grass. Brings haiku, but isn't that
just gesture? The point is no

longer to see the world through glass.
Across the adjusting sky

is a parody of sky. I don't like it either.
In the bank lot an early street-

light colors me violet.

CLASSIC

A man will rise in the middle
of the night, put a noun
where there is none. Like right now
the Segway Human Transporter.
Inventors have their patent wars.
Devices constructed only
to move us. Maybe it's obvious
things are all that's left.
Later I will drag my brother
to a film about two brothers who
walk into a big vault
and get locked inside with only one
flat soda between them
and no real way to breathe
except by drawing air through keyholes
in deposit boxes. The father
who dies earlier in the film
in shorts and sneakers returns
as a benevolent ghost
still feeling human feelings. Today
my brother and I walk
across the park following a trail of ink
droplets until the wind picks up.
Me and my brother in inclement weather.
I eat the piece of hail
he hands to me. I ask, can a poem behave
like a painkiller?
We don't have the technology yet.

REPRESENTATIVE

I couldn't remember my mother's maiden name.
The death of the author in other words.

It's May and I have to protect my checkbook in the rain.
What it says and the way I feel.

The chapter where my brother was born and moved through the branches.
You have a dream that fills the carpet, and that dream

can become like a failed crop. The sky
like a ledger. When prompted for my password I say

it's complicated. A part of the body portentously soft.
A bridge spanning here and there.

The city in which you were born. The name of your
favorite pet echoing through the house.

THE PUNCHLINES

Some have described what you and I will be as like money.

Keep quiet, let the conceit surround you.

There are dollar bills scotch-taped to deli walls.

In Point Pleasant a woman writes checks like she's in a movie.

A man carries cases of Bud.

The market absorbs the image again.

The next best economy is whatever word.

A boss walks into a break room.

Everyone's getting new smocks.

A man walks into a restroom with an accordion file full of invoices.

Everyone is in a meeting for a few days.

No one is looking for you.

A worker stares at the break room mirror for a quarter of an hour.

First of all we're running a business.

Supermarket is the subject.

The dream is to someday pay everything off.

A man walks into a duplex at night with a rebuilt compressor.

A boy walks into a refrigerator box.

A woman wakes up with 480 credit.

Everyone's clothes smell like campfire.

I am asleep in black underwear.

Everywhere now pale sunshine and droves of cars being driven to work.

I imagine my boss will be a gorgeous woman.

I please my boss with right-sounding words.

She is turning on the OPEN sign.

Like everything it is digital.

Christopher Salerno was born and raised in New Jersey and North Carolina. He has degrees from East Carolina University and Bennington College. His previous books of poems include *AORTA* (Poor Claudia, 2013), *Minimum Heroic* (Mississippi Review Poetry Prize, 2010), and *Whirligig* (Spuyten Duyvil, 2006). His chapbooks are *Automatic Teller* (Laurel Review Midwest Chapbook Prize, 2013) and *Waving Something White* (University Book Exchange, 2003). He's an Assistant Professor of English at William Paterson University where he manages the new journal, *Map Literary*. He can be reached at salerno50@hotmail.com